WHAT'S INSIDE?!
TAKE A JOURNEY THR
JAPAN'S HISTORY AND C

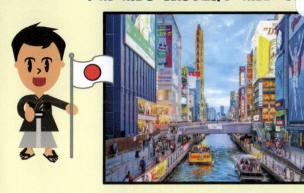

Learn about the Jomon, Muromachi & Edo Periods, Samurai, Traditional Minka Homes, Tea Ceremony, Sushi, Origami, History of the Japanese Flag, Mt. Fuji, Sumo and MORE!!!!

Kid Planet books are made in a way to help kids learn. Including traditional words and phrases!

Perfect for homeschooling or teaching someone about their heritage and other countries!

PLEASE SUBSCRIBE AND FOLLOW!

Amazon.com/author/LOGANSTOVER

Facebook.com/KIDPLANETCHILDRENSBOOKS

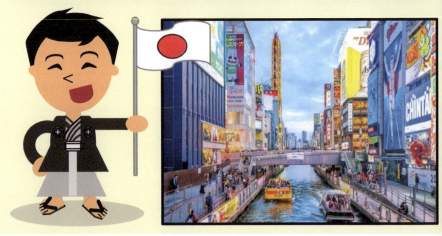

HELLO AND WELCOME TO KID PLANET, KID HISTORY! MY NAME IS KAITO!

I'm from the legendary country of Japan or Nippon-Koku. My family in I live in the southern portion of Japan in a city called Osaka. Our city is sometimes referred to as the Nation's Kitchen because we serve some of the best food in all of Japan! We're also known for our fun-loving nightlife and successful baseball team the Hanshin Tigers.

I have been told that you wanted to learn about my home country, and I'd be more than happy to give you a tour. Japan is one of the most beautiful islands in the world and has some amazing cultural locations and stories. It's a country filled with giant wrestlers, raw fish and a triple decker volcano!

LET'S LEARN ABOUT JAPAN!

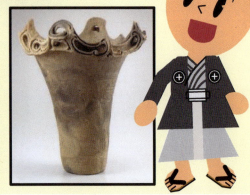

THE JOMON PERIOD!

Japan's history has often been described by it's time periods. Each period represents different cultures, people and political views. Let's start off our journey of Nipon's history with one if its earliest periods called the 'Jomon Period'.

The Jomon period is the oldest recorded history of Japan and can be dated back over fifteen thousand years! The name Jomon means patterned or colored and this is a reference to the beautiful pottery made during this time. The natives would roll soft coils of clay and stack them to form pots. After adding shells and rocks to keep the pottery strong, they were placed in hot fires to cure. Jomon period pottery is the oldest pottery that has been found in the entire world!

The Japanese natives during the Jomon period were not strong in their farming skills, and they had little to no contact with any people off the island. Instead of farming, they relied on being excellent hunters and fishers. Many Jomon fishing tools have been uncovered and are still in great condition. Scientists are amazed at the thousands of years the Jomon period artifacts have lasted considering the natives only had basic stone and wooden tools!

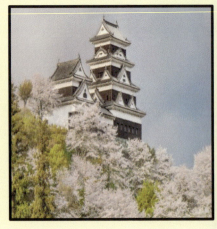

MUROMACHI & EDO PERIODS!

Let's jump ahead in our journey of Japanese history to the 'Muromachi' and 'Edo' periods. The Jomon period was known for its art and culture. However, our next time period was remembered for being the exact opposite. The Muromachi period was defined by warfare and fighting, and the Edo period represented rapid technological growth . The Muromachi period was named after the area of the city of Kyoto in which the first shogun, Takauji, set up his headquarters. A shogun is the name of a military leader of the people. That is why the Muromachi period was also known as the 'Ashikaga Period', which means the "time of military control".

Despite this time being called the 'Age of the Country at War', the Japanese culture developed some beautiful arts and important religious teachings during these times. Zen Buddhism, flower arranging, and the Japanese Tea Ceremony were all developed during these eras. During the Edo period, the first European traders arrived bringing with them their arts, foods and religions. Japan also began to establish strong connections with China and Korea, which still last to this day.

THE Samurai!

The Edo period also came to be known as the "Age of the Samurai"! A man named Tokugawa Leyasu emerged as the leader of Japan after the many years of fighting during the Muromachi period. He was appointed Shogun and established his military headquarters in the modern-day city of Tokyo or Edo. This military form of government lasted for over two hundred years, and like some of those that came before it, tried to keep Japan secluded from the rest of the world. However, even with a focus on military strength, Japanese art forms and culture still flourished. The Samurai are an example of one of Japan's more well known military art forms.

The Samurai were the Shogun's personal appointed military leaders. They were highly respected warriors that lived lives of luxury and had many privileges. The Samurai received advanced education and training in reading, mathematics and fighting. They were loyal to their appointed leaders and could be called to battle at any moment. Short times of peace during the Edo period allowed for some ingenious combinations of beautiful art and practical military applications.

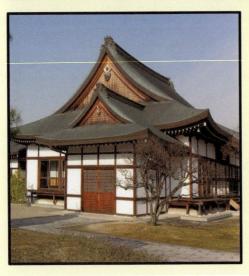
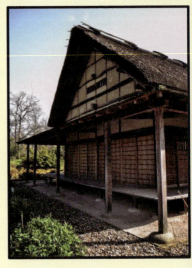

TRADITIONAL MINKA HOMES

Japan is famous for its beautiful and functional homes called 'Minka'. These homes are made in visually pleasing styles and have some very unique features. Minka homes are intended to be minimal and efficient. So, don't be surprised if you can't find an extra chair or bed! The space inside the home is arranged in ways to improve the flow of energy in a person's body and this idea of energy flow is referred to as Zen.

Traditional Japanese furniture tends to be very low to the ground and rests on a special type of flooring called 'Tatami' which is comfortable and strong. Low tables called 'Chabudai' are often used as family tables for eating and tea drinking. The tables are very basic in their form as they are meant to keep with the home's minimalistic design.

Nature also plays an important part in traditional Japanese homes. Often the entire home is built to reflect and appreciate the nature around it. Minka homes are famous for their sliding doors called 'Shoji'. The doors can slide into different formations to allow one space to serve multiple purposes. Minimal and functional was the Minka way!

JAPANESE TEA CEREMONY

All this traveling has me thirsty, and I know the perfect place we can go. Welcome to a traditional Japanese Tea Ceremony. The tea ceremony isn't a quick stop for a drink, but rather an event that can last for hours. The Japanese tea ceremony has strict protocol and rules on how the tea process takes place. The rules can be so detailed that there are often rules on what to do with your hands!

The Japanese tea ceremony is one of the most famous art forms of the Japanese culture. It was refined and perfected over five hundred years ago by a man named Sen No Rikyu. He helped form the rules and procedures that guide the tea ceremony. The rules help guide the ceremony and also it helps preserve Japanese tradition. For example, one rule is that you shouldn't dress extravagantly or smell of too much scent, so that you do not distract from the tea. Another important factor is the location of the tea drinking. Original teachings advise to enjoy tea in a garden that provides a zen feeling of calm or a dedicated room in the home for tea only. Did you ever imagine that drinking tea could be considered an art?

THE HISTORY OF SUSHI!

Chances are that you have heard of sushi as it is served all over the world. However, did you know that Japan has been perfecting the art of sushi making for over eight hundred years?

Japan's earliest sushi was referred to as 'Narezushi', which means sour tasting. Sushi was originally created as a way to preserve fish that were caught in rice paddies after floods. Unlike today's fresh sushi, the original makers fermented and stored their fish to be eaten at a later time. It was during the Edo period that people began to add vinegar and 'nori' to their sushi. Nori is the Japanese term for seaweed, and it's my favorite part!

It wasn't until 1824 that sushi was considered perfected by a man named Hanaya Yohei. He introduced high quality fresh raw fish instead and called it 'Edomae' sushi or "Tokyo Bay" sushi. Sushi today comes in mainly two forms called nigiri and maki. Nigiri sushi is made by rolling a small pack of rice and covering it with various types of seafoods. Maki sushi is created by combining ingredients inside a roll of nori and then slicing it up into individual pieces.

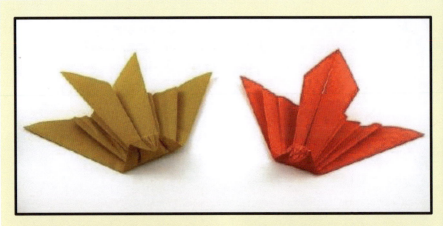

ORigami!

Let's take a moment to learn about another of Japan's famous artforms. However, this one isn't edible. It's called Origami, and it means "folding paper". The purpose of origami is to take paper and fold it into different figures and shapes. This Japanese tradition of folding paper figures dates back over one thousand years. One of the earliest figures were small butterflies called 'Ocho' and 'Meccho' and they were used to decorate special occasions like births and weddings. Each origami figure has its own meaning and purpose!

Many designs began to appear in Japan beginning in the 1800's, and one of the most famous of them is the crane. In Japanese culture, the crane is considered a mystical bird of happiness that represents long life and good fortune. Gifting of origami cranes is a long-standing tradition of Japanese culture. In fact, you can give yourself some good luck just by folding them! Japanese tradition states that you can have a wish come true, and all you have to do is fold one thousand origami cranes. One thousand? We'll have to work on those later.

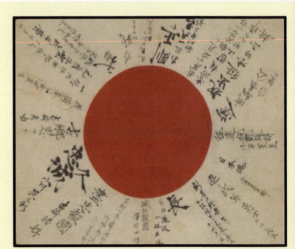

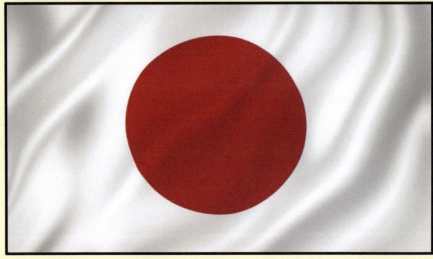

NiSSHOKi, THE JaPaNESE FLag!

Time for us to learn more about the national flag of Japan! It's name is Nisshōki or Hinomaru and it is made up of a crimson 'sun disc' on a white background. It has been used as the national flag of Japan for hundreds of years. However, it was only recently that the sun disk flag was confirmed as the Japanese national flag.

Japan is sometimes referred to as "The land of the rising sun", and this is often in reference to the national flag. The Japanese citizens honored the representations of the flag and how it symbolized their country. The red disc at the center became to known to symbolize the sun goddess, "Amaterasu". While the white background is meant to represent the honesty and integrity of the Japanese citizens.

The flag is also considered a good luck gift! Traditionally, soldiers would be given flags with writings of encouragement or prayers. They would be written around the white area of the flag for good luck as long as the writing never touched the sun disc. So, next time you hear the phrase "land of the rising sun" or see a Japanese flag with writing, you'll know what it means to the Japanese culture!

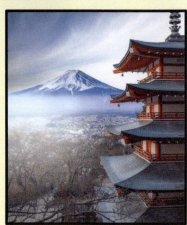

MOUNT FUJI!

We are heading from one Japanese cultural landmark to another. Welcome to Mount Fuji. This mountain stands at over 3,700 meters tall and is the seventh highest island peak in the world. It's also one of Japan's three sacred mountains along with Mt. Haku and Mt. Tate. Mt. Fuji is one of Japan's most iconic locations and has even earned a UNESCO World Heritage listing. It's been a location of pilgrimages and inspiration for paintings and poems. It was even once used as a remote secret samurai training base!

Mt. Fuji is no ordinary mountain. It's actually an active volcano! Technically speaking, it is three of them stacked on top of each other. The oldest one on the bottom is called the Komitake volcano, which has the Kofuji volcano sitting on top of it. Mt. Fuji is the most recent volcano and sits on top of the previous two. That's a lot of volcanos! The crater of Mt. Fuji is massive at a diameter of over 500 meters and a depth of over 250 meters. Fuji is still active, but it's been 300 years since erupting in 1707.

Despite Fuji being an active volcano, every year tens of thousands of adventurists take the risk of climbing the mountain. The climb itself doesn't take too long and can be completed in a day. However, the window to climb is very short due to the harsh weather conditions and lasts only from July to August. The Japanese culture respects the risks and power of the volcano as an old Japanese passage says, "someone wise will climb Mt. Fuji once in their life. Only a fool would climb it twice".

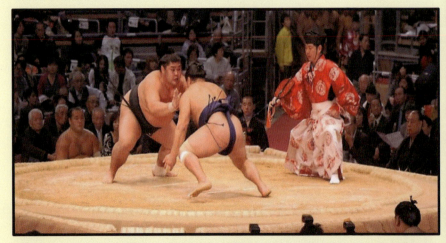

SUMO

This is a Japanese sumo hall, and it is home to Japan's national sport Sumo! It is a form of wrestling and has been a part of Japanese culture for centuries. Sumo wrestlers are large athletes that compete in matches that often only last a few moments. In fact, Sumo has no weight limit and some wrestlers grow very large. During a match, two wrestlers face each other in a sand ring called a 'Dohyo' and attempt to push each other out. The winner is the first wrestler to push their opponent out of the ring or have them touch the floor with a part of their body other than their feet. It's truly amazing to see athletes of this caliber moving with such speed and precision.

Sumo athletes live and train in specialized facilities or stables called 'Heya'. One of the most famous sumo districts is located in Tokyo and is called Ryogoku. It houses over forty stables alone! A sumo stable is professionally run, and the athletes' routines are kept very regimented. A stable master guides every part of the wrestler's lives including when they spend their free time, eat and sleep. The heya is also private and often closed to all visitors. Even if you are let in, you won't be allowed to do much more than sit quietly on the floor and observe. In addition, you will also need to be fluent in Japanese and be familiar with every traditional sumo custom. These are serious facilities that are intended to produce elite athletes. Large amounts of money are spent to maintain and train wrestlers to peak condition. Don't worry if you don't have the chance to visit a heya as everyone is invited to watch professional matches!

REVIEW

- JOMON, MUROMACHI & EDO PERIODS
- SAMURAI
- MINKA HOMES
- TEA CEREMONY
- SUSHI
- ORIGAMI
- JAPANESE FLAG
- MT. FUJI
- SUMO

LET'S REVIEW!

We learned about the Jomon, Muromachi and Edo periods. These were important time periods in which Japan's culture developed. Then we spent time with the Samurai and learned about how they were a unique combination of art and war. Function, efficiency and nature are the inspirations behind traditional minka homes. Remember to follow all the rules of the tea ceremony and don't forget to try all the types of delicious sushi! We learned about folding origami and that making a thousand cranes will bring you good luck. Now we know the meanings of the Japanese flag and the tradition of writing notes on them. If you are feeling adventurous, make sure to stop by Mt. Fuji for a climb up an active volcano. Finally, we found out that sumo wrestlers are elite athletes who train in special sumo stables!

I have had such an amazing time teaching you about Japan and I hope you have enjoyed learning!

UNTIL NEXT TIME...

WELCOME TO JAPAN!

CHECK OUT ALL OUR BOOKS!

FREE VIDEO AND NARRATION OF BOOKS ON OUR YOUTUBE PAGE!

PLEASE FOLLOW KID PLANET!

   You Tube

@STOVERVOICEOVER

AMAZON.COM/AUTHOR/LoganSTOVER

FACEBOOK.COM/KIDPLANETCHILDRENSBOOKS

ABOUT KID PLANET!

LOGAN STOVER IS THE AUTHOR AND ILLUSTRATOR OF
KID PLANET CHILDREN'S BOOKS!

HE RESIDES IN ORANGE COUNTY, CA
WITH HIS BEAUTIFUL FAMILY.

KIDS AND ADULTS LOVE LOGAN'S BOOKS FOR THEIR UNIQUE SHAPE CREATED CHARACTERS, FUN HISTORICAL STORIES, AND AMAZING REAL-LIFE PHOTOS!

Printed in Great Britain
by Amazon

21873906R00018